The Elements in Poetry

EARTH

Cherrytree Books are distributed in the United States by Black Rabbit Books
P.O. Box 3263
Mankato, MN 56002

Printed in China by WKT Company Ltd.

Library of Congress Cataloging-in-Publication Data
Poems about earth / compiled by Andrew Fusek Peters.
        p. cm. -- (The elements in poetry)
    Summary: "A collection of poetry for elementary students about the science of Earth, including
periodic elements, hibernation, plate tectonics, and more"--Provided by publisher.
    Includes index.
    ISBN 978-1-84234-520-7
    1. Earth--Juvenile poetry. 2. Nature--Juvenile poetry. 3. Four elements (Philosophy)--Juvenile poetry.
4. Children's poetry, English. I. Peters, Andrew (Andrew Fusek) II. Title. III. Series.

PR1195.E17P64 2009
821.008'09282--dc22

                                    2007048056

13-digit ISBN: 9781842345207
10-digit ISBN: 1842345206

First edition
9 8 7 6 5 4 3 2 1

First published in 2007 by Evans Brothers Ltd.
2A Portman Mansions, Chiltern Street,
London W1U 6NR, United Kingdom

Editorial: Julia Bird & Su Swallow
Design: Simon Borrough
Production: Jenny Mulvanny

Contents

Riddle

My first is in water, but isn't in air,

My second's in ocean and sea, but not there.

My third's in a river but not in a vale,

My fourth is in stream, but not moor, hill or dale.

My fifth can be seen in a ditch – not a street –

And my whole can be found under everyone's feet.

{Earth}

Alison Chisholm

Don't Tread on Worms!

I'm asking you nicely:
Please don't tread on worms –
Even though you dislike
All their wriggles and squirms.
You see, there's a great deal
About the earthworm
That deserves your regard
And respect and concern.
First, the tunnels it makes
In the darkness down there
Let into the ground
Both water and air
And it swallows each day
Dead leaves and such stuff
Along with much earth –
It can't get enough!
Then out it all comes
As nice crumbly soil –
Saving the gardener
Much back-breaking toil.
If you think about that
You'll find it confirms
The idea that you shouldn't
Be nasty to worms.

(P.S. They're food
For the birds and the fishes
Though these uses may well be
Against a worm's wishes).

Eric Finney

The Sunflower

I'm curled up, quietly waiting,
tiny in the ground.
the soil is my blanket,
I'm asleep where there's no sound.

but now the earth is warmer,
the time has come to wake,
with a yawning little shiver
and a quiver and a shake.

slowly, very slowly
out pokes my tiny shoot.
then, like a bunch of fingers
down grows my sturdy root.

stronger now, I reach up
and push for all I'm worth,
waiting for the moment
when I'll break free from the earth.

now I am uncurling
young leaves on either side
then whoosh! I'm stretching upwards
first straight and tall, then wide.

my leaves are arched like bird's wings,
they flutter in the air.
my petals are unfurling
like a plate with yellow hair.

look at me! I'm swaying
a leaning, smiling tower.
I turn my face to catch the sun,
a tall and proud sunflower.

Polly Peters

WEB OF LIFE

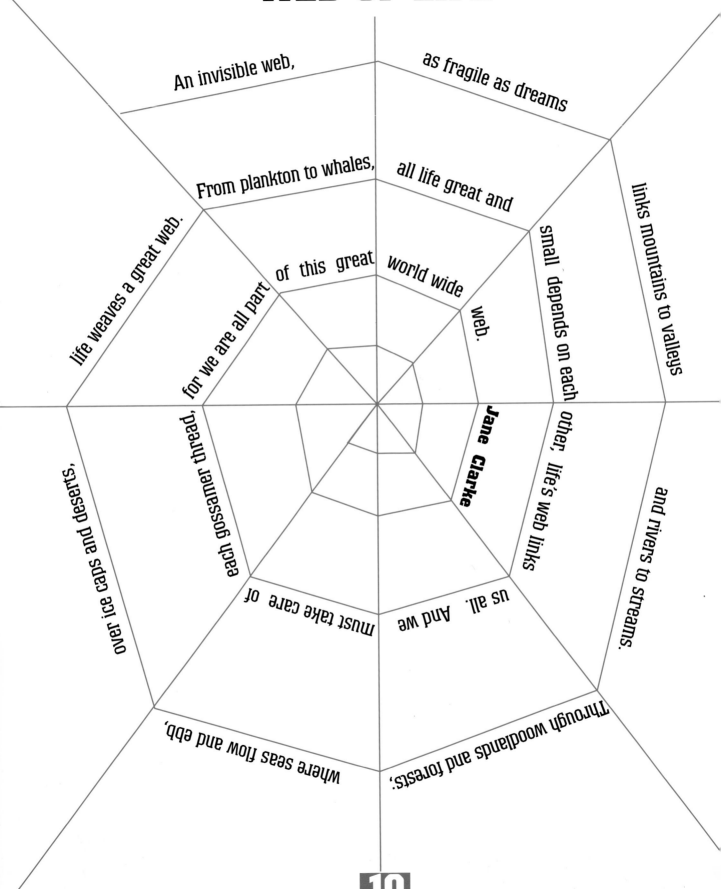

An invisible web,

as fragile as dreams

From plankton to whales,

all life great and

links mountains to valleys

life weaves a great web.

of this great

world wide

small depends on each

for we are all part

web.

Jane Clarke

other, life's web links

each gossamer thread,

over ice caps and deserts,

must take care of

And we

us all.

where seas flow and ebb,

Through woodlands and forests,

and rivers to streams.

Plate Tectonics

The crust of the earth is a lithosphere
Broken into plates,
They slide around and meet and fight
Just like a bunch of mates

But when they get together,
It can be quite titanic,
From earthquake to tsunami
And activities volcanic

When the Indian and Eurasian plates
Fought to see who's best,
This mountain of an argument
Turned into Everest!

Andrew Fusek Peters

HOW A CAVE WILL BEHAVE

Take a look at these cone-like formations,
And remember, wherever they're found,

A stalactite drips down from the ceiling.
A stalagmite grows up from the ground.

J.Patrick Lewis

Hibernation

Too cold to move
above ground
so scratch, crawl, fall
into caves under tree roots.
There
as wind blows
frost, hail, rain
falls,
beetles slow,
until the sun
winds up their six-legged
batteries again.

Lorraine Marwood

Desert Camouflage

Something shimmers in the desert,
In the burning barren land,
Something's rippling the surface
Of the dazzling desert sand.

Something's slowly stirring
As the scorched sand swirls and billows.
Something wrapped in sandy blankets,
Cushioned by plump sandy pillows.

In the shifting, drifting desert
A sun-baked sand dune wakes.
In the windswept, weathered wasteland
A sand dune snorts and shakes.

The desert sands are breathing!
It's a shimmering mirage,
A dream-drugged dromedary
Wearing desert camel-flage.

Jane Clarke

Silence

lives in the rain forests of the Amazon
Where every drop of cool rain falls.
As a thread of gossamer curtain
Parting to reveal a mime:
Spiders spinning life tales
Between giant trees;
Big brown ants readying a rich feast for their queen
Silence walks through this ageing carpet
Of muddy earth and leaves
Through a dark, endless cavern of
Translucent green
Covering each breath with a heavy blanket
of quiet. Even the Earth does not speak
as it claims an old tree
crashing
soundlessly.

Jeneen Garcia

An Elder's Prayer

O great spirit of my forest
I have nothing in my hand
But a chicken and some rice,
It's the gift of my land.
Bring us sunshine with the rains
Save my people from all pains;
When the harvest time is done
We will make a feast to you.

Bai T. Moore

EARTH

I am the Earth.
Once, forest covered my face
Like a green beard,
And great animals hunted in it.
But now men come with sharp razors
To scrape my tender skin,
Leaving nothing but cuts and sores and stubble.
Soon I will be barefaced and bald.
I'll never get used to it,
Even if it is
The latest fashion.

David Orme

The Good Earth

More precious than gold,
Some call it mud
But earth makes bodies
Bone and blood.
It grows the plants
Which feed us all
So, birds and beasts,
Both large and small
Come from earth
As humans do.
Earth has grown
Me and you.
More precious than gold,
Don't call it mud,
Call it bodies,
Bone and blood.

Marian Swinger

ASPECTS OF EARTH

It's solid ground. The stuff beneath our feet
we take for granted, packed in winter's hold,
its surface unaffected by the beat
of boots that head for home: hard, barren, cold,
a ghostly pallor. That's not death, but sleep.
Time to get up. Spring light, a shower, drive
those tiny stems, like nails; they clutch and creep
skywards, between the clods. The land's alive.
Gold glowing corn, a lurid slash of rape*
invade the shaded subtleties of green
as sun and rain fashion the soil's shape
from mud to powder, rock to plasticine.
Shifting position, keen to re-arrange
her make-up, Mother smiles. She likes a change.

Paul Francis

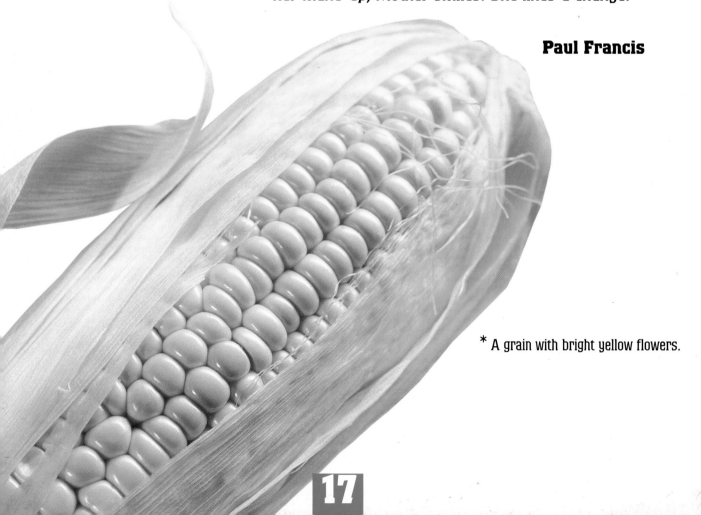

* A grain with bright yellow flowers.

GRAVITY

If it wasn't for earth's
Gravitational pull
Then objects would float up
And skies would be full
Of ripe conkers*, bombs, cow dung,
Those pencils we lose
From coat pockets, high jumpers
Like large kangaroos,
Confetti, leaves, litter,
A melee of fruit,
All those sticks thrown for puppies
And the footballs we boot.
Imagine: this planet
A much tidier place.
But think of that mess
Up in space

Rachel Rooney

* A horse chestnut.

Elemental Tea

Silverware gleams
The copper kettle steams
Boiling liquid mercury
For elemental tea
Tin toast spread
With nickel and lead
Iron titanium tablecloths
For elemental tea
Platinum pie
Golden pastries piled high
Set the chromium cutlery
For elemental tea
Tungsten teaspoons
Aluminium macaroons
Serve selenium sandwiches
For elemental tea
Unalloyed fun
Finish every cake and bun
Wash up in the kitchen zinc
After elemental tea

Catriona Tippin

Nature's Jewel

I
Now sigh
And fly down
From tree top crown
Fall and flutter, sleep,
Compost, compressed, lie deep
Years in millions are my goal,
This dream becomes a seam of coal
More time crawls by, will not be rushed
Watch as my black heart is crushed!
Transformed, my carbon weight
Meets its fiery fate
Diamonds are sharp
Sings my harp
This rare
Flare.

Andrew Fusek Peters

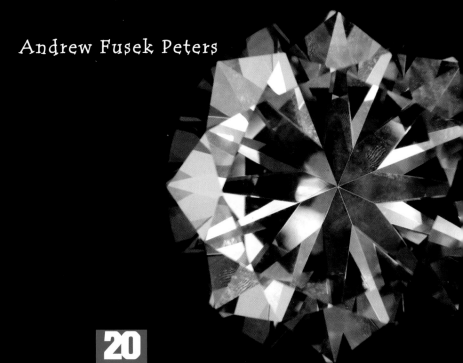

MUCKISH MOUNTAIN (THE PIG'S BACK)

Like a sleeping swine upon the skyline,
Muckish, thou art shadowed out,
Grubbing up the rubble of the ages
With your broken, granite snout.

Muckish, greatest pig in Ulster's oakwoods,
Littered out of rock and fire,
Deep you thrust your mottled flanks for cooling
Underneath the peaty mire.

Long before the Gael* was young in Ireland,
You were ribbed and old and grey,
Muckish, you have long outstayed his staying,
You have seen him swept away.

Muckish, you will not forget the people
Of the laughing speech and eye,
They who gave you name of Pig-back-mountain
And the Heavens for a sty!

Shane Leslie

*The ancient Celtic people
of Ireland. *Muc* is
Celtic for pig.

Composed upon Westminster Bridge Sept. 3, 1803

Earth has not anything to show more fair:
Dull would be he of soul who could pass by
A sight so touching in its majesty:
This City now doth, like a garment, wear
The beauty of the morning; silent, bare,
Ships, towers, domes, theatres, and temples lie
Open unto the fields, and to the sky:
All bright and glittering in the smokeless air.
Never did sun more beautifully steep
In his first splendour, valley, rock, or hill;
Ne'er saw I, never felt, a calm so deep!
The river glideth at his own sweet will:
Dear God! The very houses seem asleep;
And all that mighty heart is lying still!

William Wordsworth

AFTER THE EARTHQUAKE

Whether to cry out in answer to
My father's strangled cries
as he shifts bricks above my head,
or whether to keep silent, holding back
this dust with clamped lips. I lie
sealed in and cannot choose.

If I speak, death will steal my breath
seeping in at the mouth;
if I choose silence he may go away
and weep, and never know how close
my grave or how I longed to answer.

Someone flutes powder from my face.
I feel warm breath. My eyelids move:
Their flutter fills my eyes with grit.
Weight lifts from my chest and arms
and inch by inch I live again.

In my father's arms
I cannot find strength to haul up
words from my darkness.

Angela Topping

On the
Grasshopper and Cricket

The poetry of earth is never dead:
When all the birds are faint with the hot sun,
And hide in cooling trees, a voice will run
From hedge to hedge about the new-mown mead;
That is the Grasshopper's – he takes the lead
In summer luxury, – he has never done
With his delights; for when tired out with fun
He rests at ease beneath some pleasant weed.
The poetry of earth is ceasing never:
On a lone winter evening, when the frost
Has wrought a silence, from the stove there shrills
The Cricket's song, in warmth increasing ever,
And seems to one in drowsiness half lost,
The Grasshopper's among some grassy hills.

John Keats

COLD COMFORT

Warm giving ground.

Till the soil, plough, dig deep.
Planted seeds take root, grow and
Suck me dry.

Carved by the plough share
I get
No share
Sheared of my bounty
I give of brown peat, red earth, white clay
Black volcanic sand.

I am used and used and used
By all
But what is returned to me?

Nappies*, battery acid, nuclear waste
Plastic, polystyrene*, pvc.

Thanks, but no thanks.
Give me your sweat, spit, blood and bodies;

No more of this
Cold comfort.

Anne Maclachlan

* "Nappies" is the British term for diapers.
* Another word for styrofoam.

Digging

Between my finger and my thumb
The squat pen rests; as snug as a gun.

Under my window a clean rasping sound
When the spade sinks into gravelly ground:
My father, digging. I look down

Till his straining rump among the flowerbeds
Bends low, comes up twenty years away
Stooping in rhythm through potato drills
Where he was digging.

The coarse boot nestled on the lug, the shaft
Against the inside knee was levered firmly.
He rooted out tall tops, buried the bright edge deep
To scatter new potatoes that we picked
Loving their cool hardness in our hands.

By God, the old man could handle a spade,
Just like his old man.

My grandfather could cut more turf in a day
Than any other man on Toner's bog.
Once I carried him milk in a bottle
Corked sloppily with paper. He straightened up
To drink it, then fell to right away
Nicking and slicing neatly, heaving sods
Over his shoulder, digging down and down
For the good turf. Digging.

The cold smell of potato mold, the squelch and slap
Of soggy peat, the curt cuts of an edge
Through living roots awaken in my head.
But I've no spade to follow men like them.

Between my finger and my thumb
The squat pen rests.
I'll dig with it.

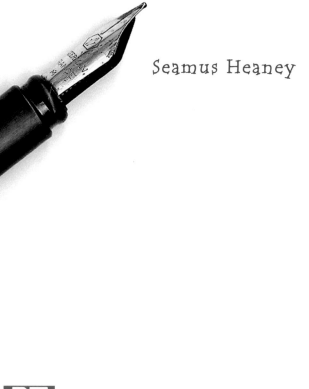

Seamus Heaney

Author Index

Acknowledgments

Alison Chisholm: "Riddle," by permission of the author.
Jane Clarke: "Web of Life" © Jane Clarke 2002 (First published in *Wild and Wonderful*, Hodder's Children's Books 2002) and "Desert Camouflage" © Jane Clarke 2006. By permission of the author.
Eric Finney: "Don't Tread on Worms," © Eric Finney. By permission of the author.
Paul Francis: "Aspects of Earth," by permission of the author.
Seamus Heaney: "Digging" from *Death of a Naturalist*. By permission of Faber and Faber.
Lorraine Marwood: "Hibernation," © Lorraine Marwood. By permission of the author.
David Orme: "Earth," © David Orme. By permission of the author.
Andrew Fusek Peters: "Nature's Jewel" and "Plate Tectonics," © Andrew Fusek Peters. By permission of the author.
Anne Maclachlan: "Cold Comfort," reprinted by permission of the author.
Polly Peters: "The Sunflower," © Polly Peters. By permission of the author.
Rachel Rooney: "Gravity," by permission of the author.
Marian Swinger: "The Good Earth," by permission of the author.
Catriona Tippin: "Elemental Tea," by permission of the author.
Angela Topping: "After the Earthquake," by permission of the author.

Every effort has been made to trace the copyright holders, but in some cases this has not proved possible. The publisher will be happy to rectify any such errors or omissions in future reprints and/or new editions.

Picture credits
Cover: © Paul Hardy/Corbis
p.6: istockphoto © Adam Blood
p.7: istockphoto © Dusty Cline
pp.8 & 9: © Tom Bean/Corbis
p.11: istockphoto © Wang Sanjun
p.12: © Mark Cooper/Corbis
p.13: © Kazuyoshi Nomachi/Corbis
p.14: istockphoto © Marje Cannon
p.15: © Chris Hellier/Corbis
p.16: istockphoto © Debbie Martin
p.17: © photocuisine/Corbis
p.18: Corbis
p.19: istockphoto © Richard Tull
p.20: istockphoto © Sheldon Gardner
p.21: © Simon Stewart
p.22: istockphoto © Geoffrey Hammond
p.23: © Reuters/Corbis
p.24: Herbert Kehrer/zefa/Corbis
p.25: istockphoto © Jim Jurica
pp.26 & 27: © Simon Borrough

THE ELEMENTS IN POETRY

Poems from the other books in this series

THE FLIGHT OF ICARUS

I rose on wings of wax,
Tracing angel tracks.

The sun called out my name
And I took reckless aim

Upward - the chosen one
First to kiss the Sun!

I started to perspire
In universal fire,

As if God struck a match
And somehow I could catch

Its light and hold it long…
I was wrong.

J.PATRICK LEWIS

Taken from **Fire**
ISBN 184234 521 4
(13-digit ISBN 978184234 521 4

Rain in the City

I had only known the splash
and the pelt and the scatter,
the gush and the gurgle of gutters
and the tumbled drums of the thunder –
until I looked downwards from an upstairs
office-block
and saw the sudden flowering
of a thousand umbrellas
in a most unlikely spring.

Anne Bell

Taken from **Water**
ISBN 184234 522 2
(13-digit ISBN 978184234 522 1

BLUEBOTTLE

Who dips, dives,
swoops out of space,
a buzz in his wings
and sky on his face;
now caught in the light,
now gone without trace,
a sliver of glass,
never still in one place?

Who's elusive as a pickpocket
lord of the flies;
who moves like a rocket,
bound for the skies?
Who's catapult, aeroplane,
always full-throttle?
Sky-diver, Jumping Jack,
comet,
bluebottle!

Judith Nicholls

Taken from **Air**
ISBN 184234 519 1
(13-digit ISBN
978184234 519 2)

About the anthologist

Andrew Fusek Peters, together with his wife Polly, has written and edited more than 45 books for young people. Their last two verse collections were nominated for the Carnegie Medal and his poems have been recorded for the Poetry Archive (www.poetryarchive.org). His collection "Mad, Bad & Dangerously Haddock" features the best of his poetry for children over the last 20 years and his anthology "Sheep Don't Go To School" has been recommended as part of the British National Curriculum. "Out of Order," his last anthology for the Evans Publishing Group, was highly praised.

"…an experienced and accomplished anthologist" "Times Educational Supplement"

"His anthologies are always surprising and interesting. He's done it again…" "Books for Keeps" five star review.

Andrew is also an experienced schools' performer, quite a good juggler, and mean didgeridoo player. Check him out on www.tallpoet.com.